D1290043

DIN🔴SAUR'S
NIGHT BEFORE
CHRISTMAS

3 1526 03982984 8

DINOSAUR'S NIGHT BEFORE CHRISTMAS

Jim Harris

PELICAN PUBLISHING COMPANY

GRETNA 2010

*To Marian, my beloved wife, for putting up with
this old T-Rex for the last twenty-seven years*

Copyright © 2010
By JHI Holdings Ltd
All rights reserved

*The word "Pelican" and the depiction of a pelican are trademarks
of Pelican Publishing Company, Inc., and are registered in the
U.S. Patent and Trademark Office.*

ISBN: 9781589808508

Printed in Singapore
Published by Pelican Publishing Company, Inc.
1000 Burmaster Street, Gretna, Louisiana 70053

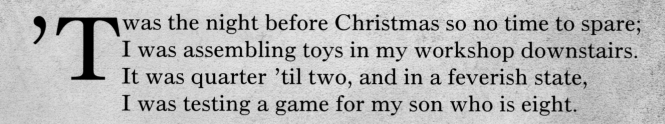

’Twas the night before Christmas so no time to spare;
I was assembling toys in my workshop downstairs.
It was quarter ’til two, and in a feverish state,
I was testing a game for my son who is eight.

When out on the lawn, there arose such a clatter,
I sprang up the stairs to see what was the matter.
And what to my wondering eyes should appear?
Well, it wasn't Saint Nick and his tiny reindeer!

By the moon that shone on the new fallen snow,
I saw what I thought was a strange UFO.
It came out of the night and flew with a roar
And was pulled by eight huge dinosaurs.

Now, the driver wasn't little, lively, or quick!
He looked more like a scrooge than good ol' St. Nick!
Like thunderbolts flashing, his coursers they came,
And he growled and he howled and he called them
by name:

Now Crusher, now Splinter, now Smasher, and Fang,
On Biter, on Cracker, on Stomper, on Slang!
To the top of the porch, to the top of the wall,
We'll dash it and smash it and flatten it all!

And then a loud crash I heard on the roof—
'Twas the stomping and clawing from each
  monster's hoof.
I'm braver than most, but in the closet I hid
When a T-Rex in red down the chimney-flue slid.

His stomach, it wagged, and his face held a sneer,
And his teeth were sharp—like long pointed
  spears.
Then a wink of his eye and a twist of his head,
And I knew he had seen me. "Oh, bother!" I said.

He spoke not a word but went right to his work
And ripped off my door with one great big jerk.
Then opening his mouth, he popped me right in,
Pulled out a hanky, and dabbed off his chin.

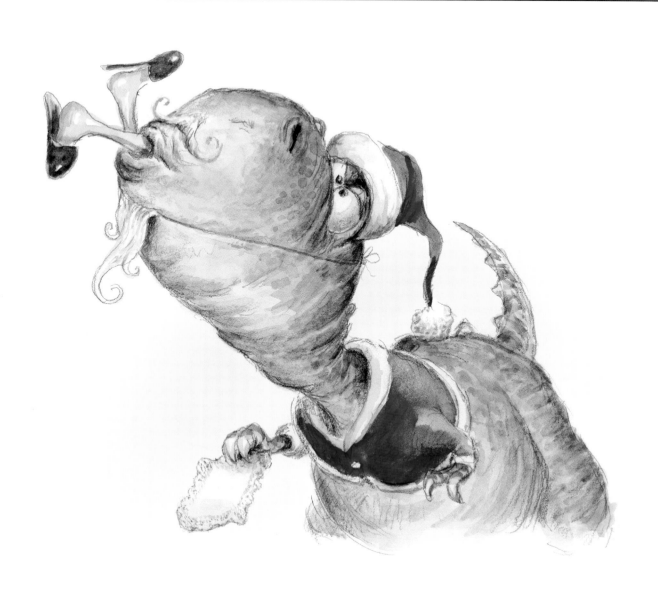

Like a greasy French fry I slid down his
  throat
'Til I splashed in his stomach and started
  to float.
"Hello!" said a voice, and it gave me a pause,
For there in a corner was ol' Santy Claus!

"I'm sorry," said Santa, "my fault I'm afraid,
But a child wrote a letter—in a very polite way—
And asked for a DINO to keep as a pet . . .
(Said he'd feed it each day, if he didn't forget).

"How *could* I deny a request made like that?
So I poured some old chemicals into a vat,
Stirred in some powder from fossilized bones,
And before I could sneeze, I'd created some
   clones!"

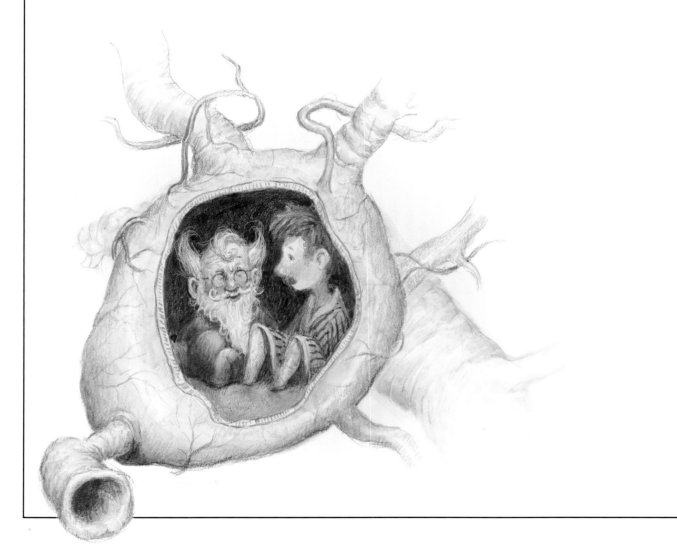

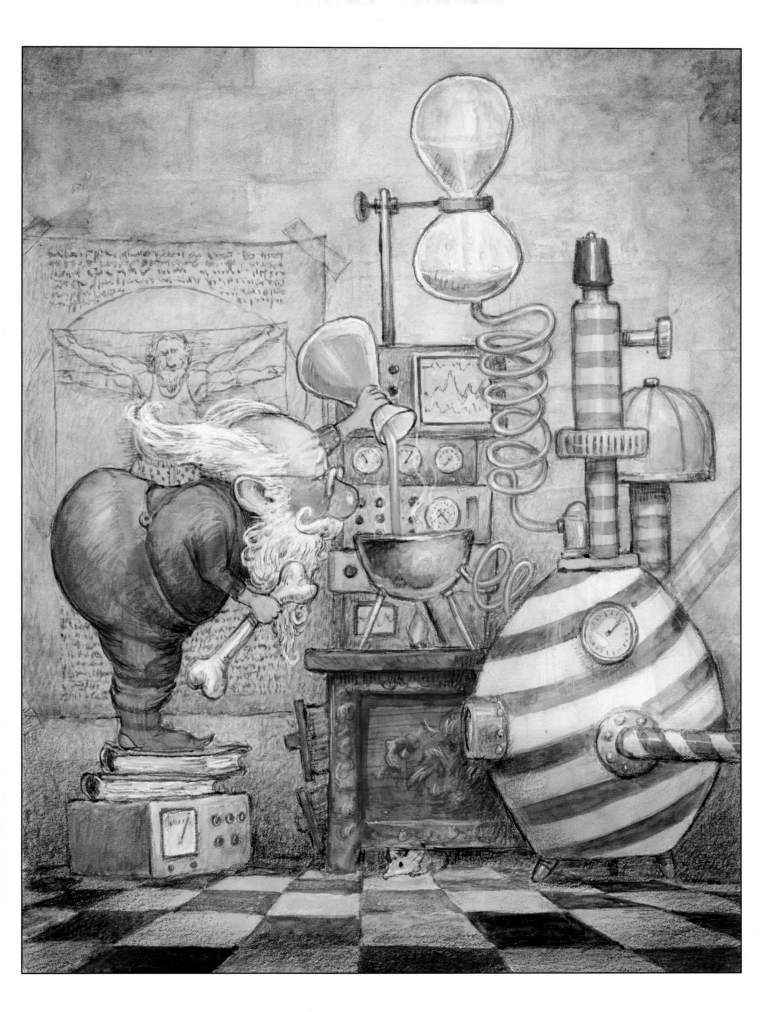

"And just like a movie where the scientist is mad,
I found I'd made monsters that were badder than bad.
Like hound dogs, they chased me around the North
   Pole
'Til T-Rex had caught me and swallowed me whole!

"Then taking my place, Rex hitched up my sleigh,
And with a growl and a howl, they flew on their way.
They've circled the globe finding nice girls and boys,
Gobbling their treats and stealing their toys!"

Santa's story was sad . . . but what could I do?
So I popped in some gum, and I started to
  chew.
"Here, Santa," I said, then blew a big bubble.
"That's nothing," he said, "I'll blow one that's
  double!"

His bubble stretched out and covered his nose.
"Not bad," I said, "but I'll cover my toes."
So I chewed real fast and started to puff,
Just hoping my bubble would grow big enough.

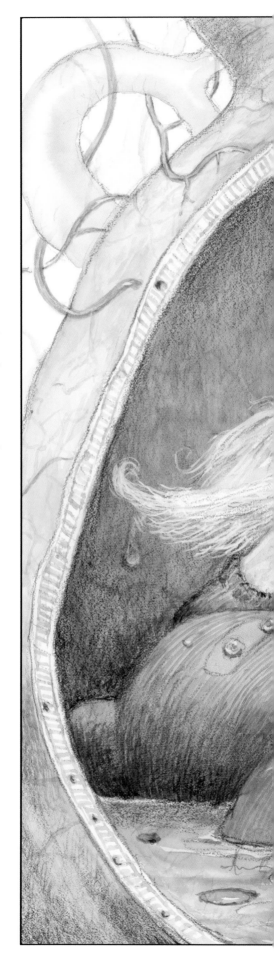

We puffed and puffed as our bubbles grew,
And the two of our bubbles stuck together like glue
Into one giant bubble that filled Rex's belly
And made him feel sick—like he ate too much jelly.

He rolled on the floor, holding onto his sides,
Giving Santa and me some pretty rough rides!
"It must have been someone I ate," T-Rex moaned,
"And it seems to me like they've suddenly grown!"

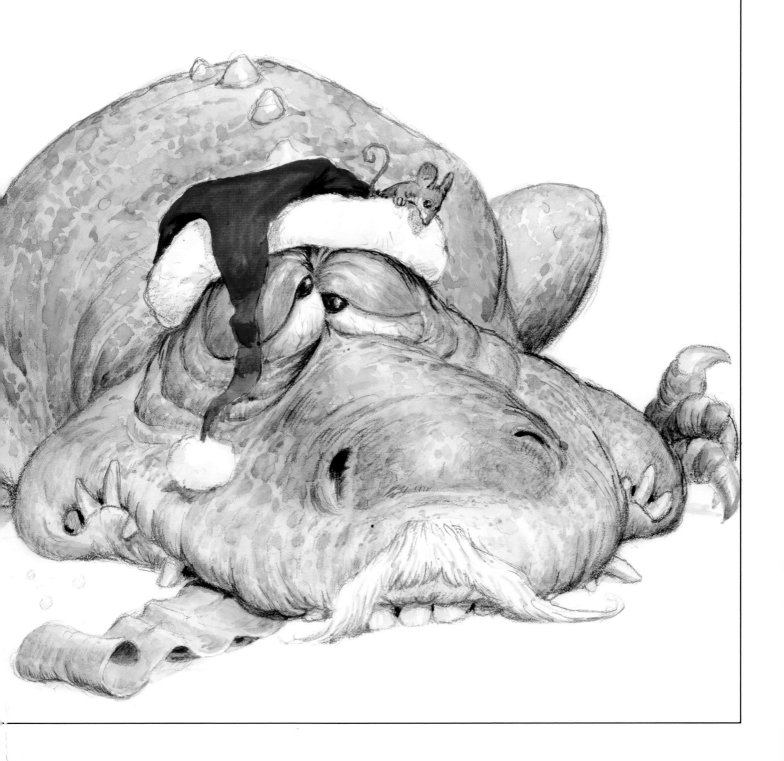

Then Rex gave a BURP that shook the whole block,
And we both popped out like two jacks in a box.
The T-Rex frowned when he saw Santa there. . . .
He was dripping with slime in his underwear!

"T-Rex!" cried Santa, "your time has come."
(As he made some adjustments to the video gun.)
But Rex roared and charged before Santa could
    shoot,
So he tossed me the gun as he ran from the brute.

They knocked down the tree and dashed through
 the hall;
They ran through the kitchen and the living-
 room wall.
Seventeen times, Santa led him my way,
But I missed every time, I'm sorry to say.

Santa was slowing; he was getting real tired.
He was huffing and puffing like a fish that's
 expired.
Then, "Dad," said a voice, from behind me this
 time,
"That's not how you shoot the X.O.K.9."

Mikey plucked up the gun and aimed down
  the sight.
There was a thundering blast and a streak of
  green light.
"That's great!" I said. "You hit him first try . . .
But now aim for the Rex as *he* passes by."

Mikey aimed once again, and there was a terrible
  boom.
When the smoke finally cleared and we could
  see the whole room,
There was nothing left where the T-Rex had been
'Cept a dinosaur toy made of plastic and tin.

A Steg on the roof must have heard all the noise,
'Cause he crept down to look and to snatch a
few toys!
When he saw 'ol Santa, he picked up the chase
But met his demise, thanks to Mikey the Ace.

Then came a Raptor and Brachiosaur . . .
Plus MASS-o-spon-DY-lus and four reptiles more!
They were very ill-tempered—nasty and mean,
But Mikey got them all—he was a toy-making
machine.

"Wow," Mikey said, "that's the bestest game ever!
Can I play it again? I could do even better."
"Ho, NO!" Santa laughed. "You *just* nicked my boot . . .
Or I'd be a toy in a Santa Claus suit!"

Then Santa sat down and said, "Now I'm confused.
My reindeer aren't here. So what can I do?"
Mikey smiled at Santa and opened a chest
And grabbed up some toys—his favorite, his best!

"These dinos are ones that I've had since brand new.
I promise they're good. What you say they will do.
They're just what you need to pull your big sleigh
(But give them some cookies and milk on the way)."

Before Santa could answer, Mikey picked up
  the gun
And flipped on a switch 'til it glowed like the sun.
He aimed at his toys and slowly at first,
Then faster they grew, with each trigger burst.

'Til finally, much taller than our chandelier,
They raced out the door—as dino-reindeer!
Then up to the roof they flew with a bound
And hitched themselves up with the harness
    they found.

"Well, well," Santa laughed, "I suppose they *will*
    do . . .
Since I can't catch a taxi . . . and I'm *quite*
    overdue.
There's only one thing . . . this little red suit
Ain't fit for the public, despite being cute."

So I scrounged up some clothes and a pair of
    old shoes.
"These stripes," I announced, "will look perfect
    on you."
"Why, thanks," Santa said, "you're awfully kind . . .
(Though they are a bit snug . . . on my ample
    behind.)"

"Don't worry," I told him, "you'll manage all
    right . . .
Besides, you'll just need them for Christmas
    Eve night."
So laying a finger aside of his nose
And giving a nod, up the chimney he rose.

But I heard him exclaim ere he drove out of
   sight . . .
"They've RIPPED!
I *knew* these pants were too tight!"